Sprout new Spelling shoots with CGP!

If you're looking for springtime spelling practice, this brilliant Daily Practice book from CGP will help pupils' spelling skills blossom beautifully!

Inside, you'll find a page of spelling practice for every school day of the spring term, covering vital skills from the Year 2 curriculum.

Easy-to-follow examples mean it's perfect for practice wherever you are — at home, at school or frolicking with the lambs!

What CGP is all about

Our sole aim here at CGP is to produce the highest quality books — carefully written, immaculately presented and dangerously close to being funny.

Then we work our socks off to get them out to you — at the cheapest possible prices.

Contents

☑ Use the tick boxes to help keep a record of which tests have been attempted.

Week 1
- ☑ Day 1 1
- ☑ Day 2 2
- ☑ Day 3 3
- ☑ Day 4 4
- ☑ Day 5 5

Week 2
- ☑ Day 1 6
- ☑ Day 2 7
- ☑ Day 3 8
- ☑ Day 4 9
- ☑ Day 5 10

Week 3
- ☑ Day 1 11
- ☑ Day 2 12
- ☑ Day 3 13
- ☑ Day 4 14
- ☑ Day 5 15

Week 4
- ☑ Day 1 16
- ☑ Day 2 17
- ☑ Day 3 18
- ☑ Day 4 19
- ☑ Day 5 20

Week 5
- ☑ Day 1 21
- ☑ Day 2 22
- ☑ Day 3 23
- ☑ Day 4 24
- ☑ Day 5 25

Week 6
- ☑ Day 1 26
- ☑ Day 2 27
- ☑ Day 3 28
- ☑ Day 4 29
- ☑ Day 5 30

Week 7
- ☑ Day 1 31
- ☑ Day 2 32
- ☑ Day 3 33
- ☑ Day 4 34
- ☑ Day 5 35

Week 8
- ☑ Day 1 36
- ☑ Day 2 37
- ☑ Day 3 38
- ☑ Day 4 39
- ☑ Day 5 40

Week 9

- ☑ Day 1 41
- ☑ Day 2 42
- ☑ Day 3 43
- ☑ Day 4 44
- ☑ Day 5 45

Week 10

- ☑ Day 1 46
- ☑ Day 2 47
- ☑ Day 3 48
- ☑ Day 4 49
- ☑ Day 5 50

Week 11

- ☑ Day 1 51
- ☑ Day 2 52
- ☑ Day 3 53
- ☑ Day 4 54
- ☑ Day 5 55

Week 12

- ☑ Day 1 56
- ☑ Day 2 57
- ☑ Day 3 58
- ☑ Day 4 59
- ☑ Day 5 60

Answers 61

Published by CGP

ISBN: 978 1 78908 829 8

Editors: Keith Blackhall, Tom Carney, Rachel Craig-McFeely, Gabrielle Richardson

With thanks to Andy Cashmore and Juliette Green for the proofreading.

With thanks to Lottie Edwards for the copyright research.

Cover and Graphics used throughout the book © www.edu-clips.com

Printed and bound by Bell and Bain Ltd, Glasgow.
Based on the classic CGP style created by Richard Parsons.

Text, design, layout and original illustrations© Coordination Group Publications Ltd. (CGP) 2021
All rights reserved.

Photocopying this book is not permitted, even if you have a CLA licence.
Extra copies are available from CGP with next day delivery • 0800 1712 712 • www.cgpbooks.co.uk

How to Use this Book

- This book contains 60 pages of daily spelling practice.

- We've split them into 12 sections — that's roughly one for each week of the Year 2 Spring term.

- Each week is made up of 5 pages, so there's one for every school day of the term (Monday – Friday).

- Each page should take about 10 minutes to complete.

- The words tested are suitable for the Year 2 English curriculum. New words and sounds are gradually introduced through the book.

- The pages increase in difficulty as you progress through the book.

- Answers can be found at the back of the book.

- Each page looks something like this:

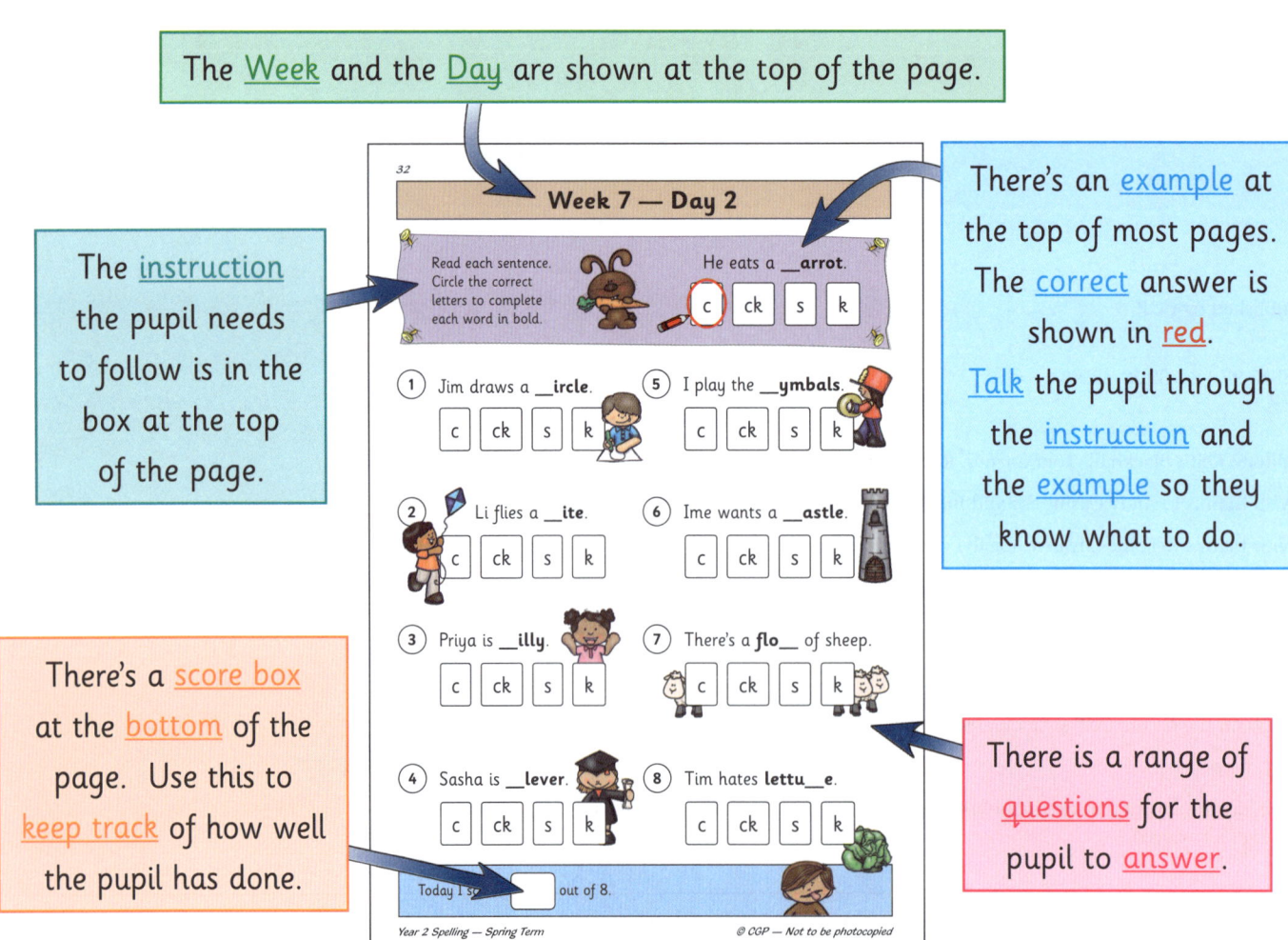

Week 1 — Day 1

Draw a line to make a compound word. Then draw another line to the matching picture.

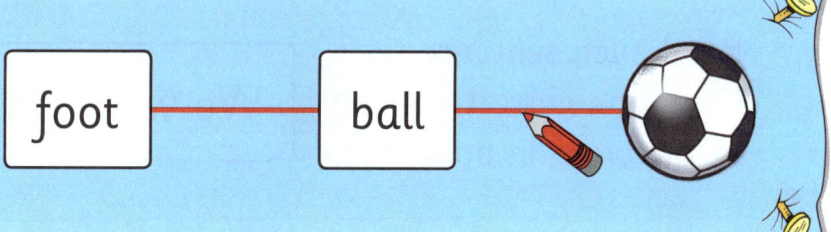

1. star — flower
2. sun — hog
3. wind — fish
4. bird — board
5. wheel — mill
6. hedge — cage
7. white — chair

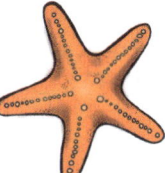

Today I scored ☐ out of 7.

Week 1 — Day 2

Read each sentence. Circle the correct spelling of the word in bold.

We write on **(papur)** / **paper** .

1) My favourite **person** / **purson** is Jake.

2) Jake is a diamond **minerr** / **miner** .

3) He loves going **underground** / **underrground** .

4) Jake found a **herd** / **herrd** of sheep in his mine.

5) They were looking for **water** / **watur** .

6) Jake **coverred** / **covered** their heads with helmets.

7) He fed them grass when they got **nervous** / **nurvous** .

Today I scored ☐ out of 7.

Week 1 — Day 3

Put a ✔ in the box if the word is spelt correctly.
Put a ✘ if it is not spelt correctly.

clowd ✘

1.  town ☐
2. shouer ☐
3.  crowd ☐
4.  owch ☐
5.  howl ☐

6. lowd ☐
7. touel ☐
8. arownd ☐
9. bouncy ☐
10. mountain ☐

Today I scored ☐ out of 10.

Week 1 — Day 4

Fill in the gap with 'or', 'ore', 'aw' or 'au' to complete each word.

th...or...n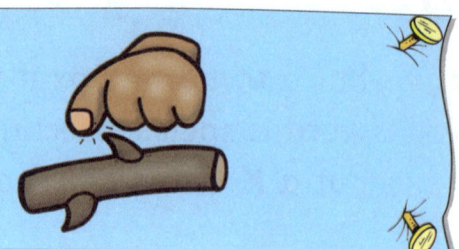

1) ac.........n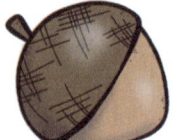

2) str.........

3) sn.........

4) h.........se

5) s.........ce

6) tract.........

7) h.........nt

8) squ.........k

9) ....tumn

10) f.........head

Today I scored ☐ out of 10.

Week 1 — Day 5

Read each sentence. Write the correct spelling of the word in bold.   I went for a walk in my **nue** boots. ......new......

1. I saw a **heuf** print in the woods. ....

2. It belonged to a friendly **mewse**. ....

3. He came and **choowed** on my jumper. ....

4. I stood still as a **statew**. ....

5. Then he left and ran out of **vue**. ....

6. I called for **rescoo** because I was lost. ....

7. A kind **rewster** led me home. ....

8. My mum made me **stoo** for tea. ....

Today I scored ☐ out of 8.

Week 2 — Day 1

Colour the picture next to the word that is spelt correctly.

1. shi / shy
2. dry / drie
3. spigh / spy
4. cri / cry
5. reply / repligh
6. terrifie / terrify

Today I scored ☐ out of 6.

Week 2 — Day 2

Draw lines to match the words to the correct missing letter. Each word should match the picture shown.

1. pie_e
2. pur_e
3. _yclist

c

s

4. di_e
5. _ilent

6. poli_e
7. _ircus
8. pen_il
9. _eal
10. _yrup

Today I scored ☐ out of 10.

Week 2 — Day 3

Read each sentence. Circle the correct spelling of the missing word.

The egg has a ____ .   crac   (crack)

1) I wore a ____ to the ball.   masc   mask

2) Yusuf opens the ____ .   can   kan

3) Luke is very ____ .   cind   kind

4) Emily is ____ .   stuk   stuck

5) I'm scared of the ____ .   dark   darck

6) The ____ takes off.   roket   rocket

7) Where is the key for the ____ ?   lock   loc

8) Julia found a ____ .   koin   coin

Today I scored ☐ out of 8.

Week 2 — Day 4

Add either 'k' or 'g' to the words in bold to complete the sentences.

He is a brave ...k...**night**.

1) The ....**nat** buzzed around Joe's ear.

2) I ....**nelt** down to look under the desk.

3) Radhika ....**nitted** a colourful scarf.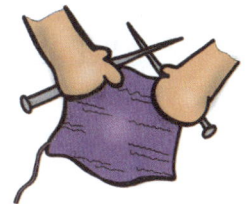

4) We don't ....**now** where we are.

5) Mehdi's garden is full of ....**nomes**.

6) The sailor tied a ....**not** in the rope.

7) Erin grazed her ....**nuckles** when she fell over.

8) The beaver ....**naws** on the log.

9) I turned the squeaky **door**.......**nob**.

Today I scored ☐ out of 9.

Week 2 — Day 5

Read each sentence. Write the correct spelling of the word in bold.

I picked up the **parcil**.   ...parcel...

1) My **uncel** is an artist. ....

2) Aqsa is a **locil** sculptor. ....

3) I sew with a **needal**. ....

4) Becky made a **modul**. ....

5) Bill made **severel** pots. ....

6) Lula is a good **pupul**. ....

7) I painted a picture of an **eagil**. ....

Today I scored [ ] out of 7.

Week 3 — Day 1

Read each sentence. Circle the correct spelling of the word in bold.

Anna **marries** / **marrys** Joe.

① The **boyes** / **boys** are wearing suits.

② Anna is holding **daisys** / **daisies** .

③ Joe **saies** / **says** that he loves Anna.

④ Anna tells **stories** / **storys** about Joe.

⑤ Anna **crys** / **cries** with joy.

⑥ Everyone **parties** / **partys** after the meal.

⑦ Christine **plays** / **plaies** the guitar.

⑧ Everyone **enjoys** / **enjoies** themselves.

Today I scored ☐ out of 8.

Week 3 — Day 2

Look at the word in the first box. Write the correct spelling of the word when the suffix in the second box is added to it.

juicy ➕ est

..juiciest..

1. icy ➕ er

....

2. dry ➕ ing

....

3. lazy ➕ est

....

4. apply ➕ ed

....

5. worry ➕ ing

....

6. reply ➕ ed

....

7. buy ➕ ing

....

8. angry ➕ er

....

9. hurry ➕ ing

....

10. deny ➕ ed

....

Today I scored ☐ out of 10.

Week 3 — Day 3

Read each sentence. Circle the letters that are missing from the word in bold.

 I opened the ___**appers**.

1) It is ___**aining** lots outside. | wr | r |

2) The dog is very ___**inkly**. | wr | r |

3) Ben ___**ote** his friend a note. | wr | r |

4) She ___**iggled** into the tiny space. | wr | r |

5) Jeni and Ama ___**ace** each other. | wr | r |

6) The queen ___**uled** the kingdom. | wr | r |

7) We explore the **ship**___**eck**. | wr | r |

Today I scored ☐ out of 7.

Week 3 — Day 4

Fill in the gap using the word in the box.
The spelling of the word will need to change.

Hetty ....**us**....**ed** up all the paint. | use

1. The nurse is very ....**ing**. | care

2. Kit is being too ....**y**. | noise

3. They ....**ed** surfing. | love

4. I want to be a ....**er**. | write

5. Duong is the ....**est** boy I know. | nice

6. The film is ....**y**. | scare

7. My mum is a ....**er**. | bake

8. Seb likes ....**ing** his bike. | ride

Today I scored ☐ out of 8.

Week 3 — Day 5

Read each sentence. Write the correct spelling of the word in bold.

It was the **hotest** day of summer. ....hottest....

1) Elena was **swiming** in the pool. ....

2) Zak was **runing** around. ....

3) Zak tried to run **fastter**. ....

4) His dad was **sittng** nearby. ....

5) "The floor is **slipy**," warned Elena. ....

6) Suddenly, Zak **trripped** over. ....

7) His dad **grabed** him. ....

8) Zak **stopd** being silly after that! ....

Today I scored ☐ out of 8.

Week 4 — Day 1

Read each sentence. Circle the correct spelling of the word in bold.

Put the potato in the **oven** / **uven** .

1) Would you like **another** / **anuther** biscuit?

2) We'll go to the park on **Sunday** / **Sonday** .

3) My **muther** / **mother** is calling me.

4) Your **brother** / **bruther** plays golf well.

5) I **wunder** / **wonder** what they'll do next.

6) The scientists made an exciting **discovery** / **discuvery** .

7) On **Munday** / **Monday** , I went shopping.

8) We will **uncover** / **uncuver** the truth.

Today I scored ☐ out of 8.

Week 4 — Day 2

Fill in the gap with either 'al' or 'all' to complete each word.

t.**all**.

1) c..........ing

2) st..........k

3) w..........ker

4) sm..........est

5) basketb..........

6) f..........ing

7) ch..........k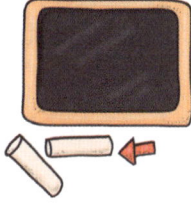

8) t..........king

9) ....most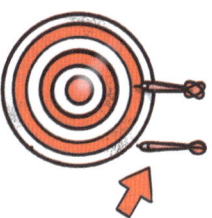

10) w..........paper

Today I scored ☐ out of 10.

Week 4 — Day 3

Read each sentence. Circle the letters missing from the word in bold.

Amir crossed the **bri**___.   ge | (dge)

1) That **he**___ is moving.   ge | dge

2) A tail is poking round the **e**___.   ge | dge

3) I hope the **ca**___ is locked.   ge | dge

4) The shark is **lar**___**r** than me.   ge | dge

5) Her **ba**___ is very shiny.   ge | dge

6) The bags **bul**___ with our shopping.   ge | dge

7) Will it all fit in the **fri**___?   ge | dge

Today I scored ___ out of 7.

Week 4 — Day 4

Read each pair of words. Put a **tick** in the box next to the word that is spelt correctly.

gnome ✓
knome

1. gnife
   knife
   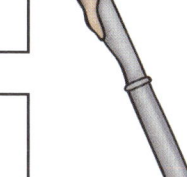

2. gnawed
   knawed

3. gnitting
   knitting

4. gnock
   knock

5. gnee
   knee

6. gnash
   knash

7. gnotted
   knotted

8. gnarled
   knarled

Today I scored ☐ out of 8.

Week 5 — Day 1

Read each sentence. Circle the letters that are missing from the word in bold.

There was once a **qu___n** called Clare.

ea | igh | (ee)

1 She had very strange **f___t**.

igh | ee | ea

2 They were the colour of **p___s**.
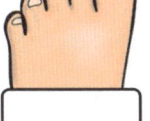

ee | ea | igh

3 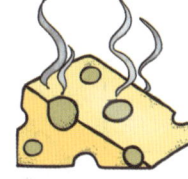 They smelt like **ch___se**.

ea | ie | ee

4 They were shaped like **p___s**!

ie | igh | ee

5 One day, **kn___ts** came to the castle.

igh | ee | ea

6  They wanted to **st___l** some gold.

ie | ea | ee

7 Clare's toes gave them a **fr___t**!

igh | ie | ea

8 They ran away into the **n___t**.

ee | ea | igh

Today I scored [ ] out of 8.

Week 5 — Day 2

Read each pair of words. Put a **tick** in the box next to the word that is spelt correctly.

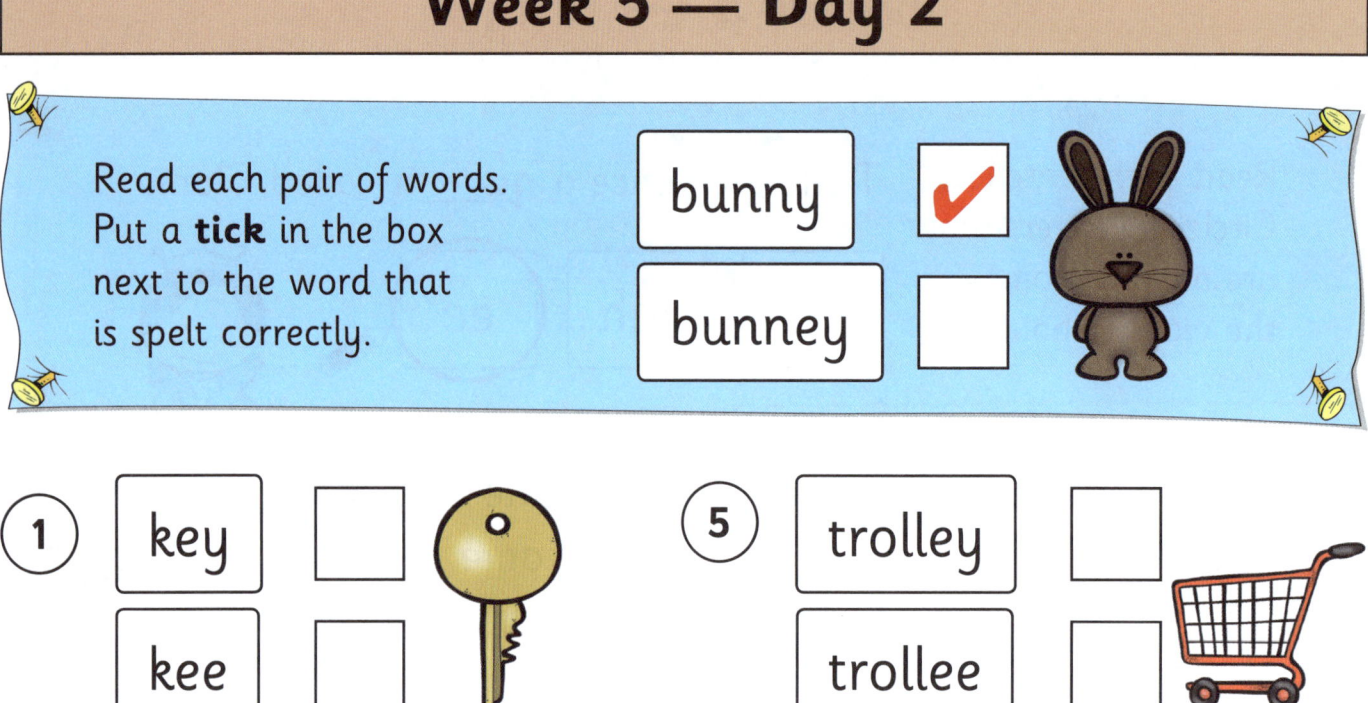

1. key / kee

2. sea / sey

3. honi / honey

4. baby / babie

5. trolley / trollee

6. monki / monkey

7. turkey / turkie

8. hockee / hockey

Today I scored ☐ out of 8.

Week 5 — Day 3

Look at the pictures. Fill in the gap with either '**er**', '**ir**' or '**ur**'.   hamm..**er**..

1 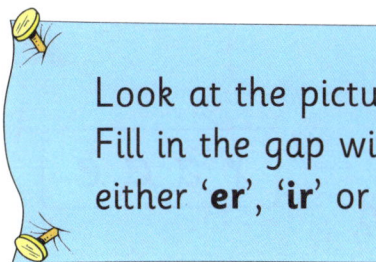 f........

2 fing........

3  sh.......t

4 tig........

5   d.......t

6  st........

7 t........nip

8 lobst........

9 flow........

10 s........prise

Today I scored ☐ out of 10.

Week 5 — Day 4

Look at the pictures. Complete the missing word in each sentence using the letters in the box.

 Erik has a bushy **b**.eard. .   r̶ a̶ d̶ e̶

1) Vikings **w**.................... shiny helmets.      r a e

2)  Leif has a big, pointy **s**.................... .   e r a p

2) Frode has lovely **h**.................... .      i a r

4) They camp **n**.................... forests.   e r a

5) They need to be **a**.................... of wolves.      w e a r

6)  Rolf **h**.................... a loud growl.   a s r e

Today I scored [ ] out of 6.

Week 5 — Day 5

Colour in each square where the word is spelt correctly to find the path to the exit.

house	ful
(yellow)	

In ↓

people	lyk	agayn	sum	tooday	luv
our	push	thort	werk	eny	thay
skool	said	watr	friend	were	once
mowse	eyes	yu	what	littel	where
Misster	because	speak	poor	heer	please
owt	hoo	hav	seys	cumm	ask

→ Out

Today I scored ☐ out of 15.

Week 6 — Day 1

Circle 'yes' or 'no' to show whether each word is spelt correctly.

funy | yes | (no)

1. skimming | yes | no

2. luckky | yes | no

3. climbbed | yes | no

4. chatty | yes | no

5. choped | yes | no

6. picked | yes | no

7. smartter | yes | no

8. scrubing | yes | no

Today I scored ☐ out of 8.

Week 6 — Day 2

Read each sentence. Circle the letters that are missing from the word in bold.

Rob mows the **l__n**. [aw] [au]

1) I think I **s__** a ghost! [aw] [or]

2) Lucy **h__ls** herself up the tree. [au] [aw]

3) The boat sailed into the **p__t**. [or] [au]

4) Joel has the highest **sc__**. [aw] [ore]

5) Samara **f__got** her book. [or] [aw]

6) The tiger has sharp **cl__s**. [aw] [au]

7) Who is your favourite **__thor**? [au] [or]

8) The weather **f__cast** was bad. [ore] [or]

Today I scored [ ] out of 8.

Week 6 — Day 3

Draw lines to match each word to the letter that is missing. Each word should match the picture shown.

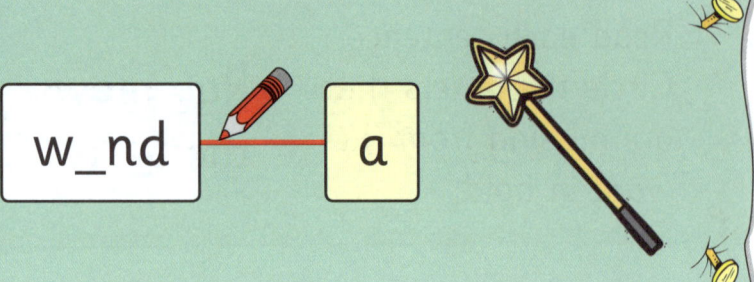

1. 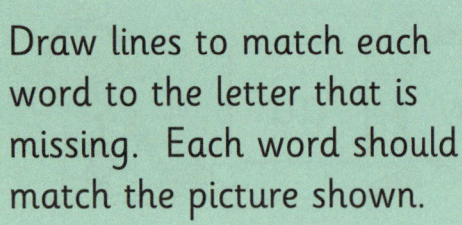 w_tch

5. w_sp

2.  f_x

o

6. sw_n

3.  h_p

7. squ_d

a

4.  qu_lity

8. f_llow

Today I scored ☐ out of 8.

Week 6 — Day 4

Read each sentence. Fill in the gap with either '**le**', '**el**', '**al**' or '**il**'.

There is a sna...il... in the garden.

1) I hide under the ta....... .

2)  Pip is in his kenn....... .

3) My favourite anim....... is a hippo.

4)  Lois found a jew....... .

5) He pressed the ped....... .

6) 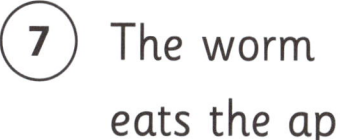 The train entered the tunn....... .

7) The worm eats the app....... .

8) I saw a cam....... .

9)  I'm learning to jugg....... .

10) The holes in noses are nostr.......s .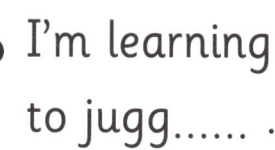

Today I scored ☐ out of 10.

Week 6 — Day 5

Use the sentences and pictures to help you fill in the missing letters in the boxes below.

My coat is **bl__**.

| b | l | u | e |

1. **N__n** means midday.

| N | | | n |

2. I tightened the **scr__**.

| s | c | r | | |

3. The **g__se** flapped its wings.

| g | | | s | e |

4. Joy **gl__d** her work into her book.

| g | l | | | d |

5. The ship's **cr__** said, "Ahoy!"

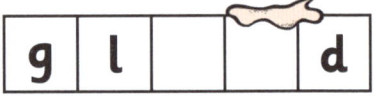

| c | r | | |

6. Kemal searched for **cl__s**.

| c | l | | | s |

Today I scored ☐ out of 6.

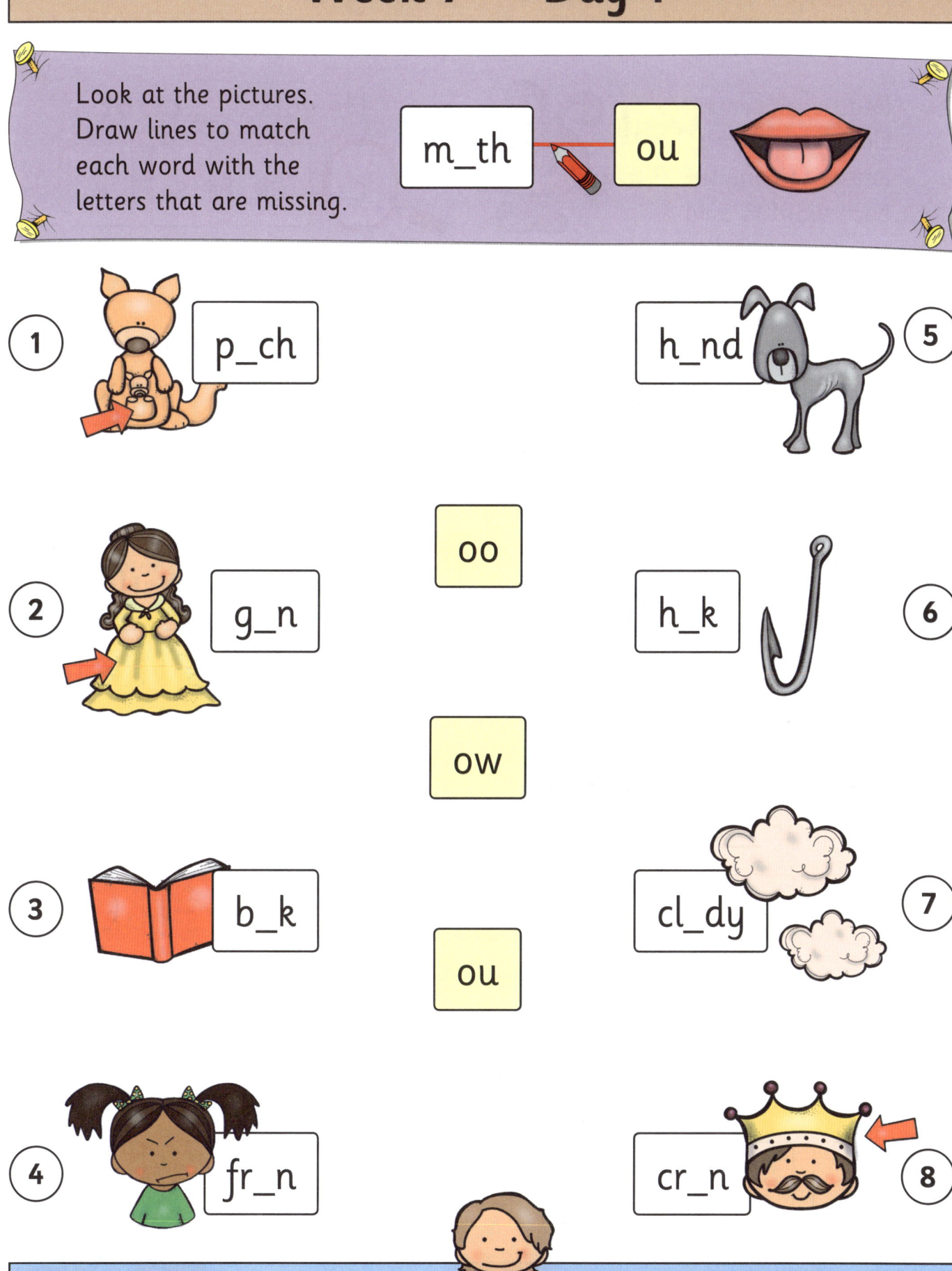

Week 7 — Day 2

Read each sentence. Circle the correct letters to complete each word in bold.

He eats a __arrot.
(c) ck s k

1. Jim draws a __ircle.
   c ck s k

2. Li flies a __ite.
   c ck s k

3. Priya is __illy.
   c ck s k

4. Sasha is __lever.
   c ck s k

5. I play the __ymbals.
   c ck s k

6. Ime wants a __astle.
   c ck s k

7. There's a **flo__** of sheep.
   c ck s k

8. Tim hates **lettu__e**.
   c ck s k

Today I scored ☐ out of 8.

Week 7 — Day 3

Read each pair of sentences. Tick the sentence where the word in bold is spelt correctly.

Sam travels the **world**. ✓
Sam travels the **werld**. ☐

1. Saul is **wurking** hard. ☐
   Saul is **working** hard. ☐

2. Cleo likes using big **words**. ☐
   Cleo likes using big **werds**. ☐

3. The **workbook** is exciting. ☐
   The **werkbook** is exciting. ☐

4. That gem is **wurthless**. ☐
   That gem is **worthless**. ☐

5. We **worship** in the temple. ☐
   We **wirship** in the temple. ☐

6. The rain is **wurse** today. ☐
   The rain is **worse** today. ☐

7. His actions are **werthy** of praise. ☐
   His actions are **worthy** of praise. ☐

Today I scored ☐ out of 7.

Week 7 — Day 4

Complete each word so that it matches the picture shown. Fill in the gaps using letters from the boxes. Only use each pair of letters once.

..sl..urp

| sm | sh | sc | sp | sw | sn | sk | sl |

1)  ....ap

2)  ....ice

3) ....ider

4)  ....ream

5) blu..........

6) ....eep

7)  ....ate

8) ....oke

Today I scored ☐ out of 8.

Week 8 — Day 1

Read each sentence. Circle the correct spelling of the missing word.

It was the middle of ____.   (July)   Juli

1) I was in ___ garden.   mai   my

2) It was warm and ___.   dry   drigh

3) A ___ fluttered past.   butterflie   butterfly

4) I could not believe my ___!   ays   eyes

5) I wanted to ___ and catch it.   try   tri

6) It was too ___ and it flew away.   sly   slie

7) It must have been ___!   shigh   shy

8) I wanted to ___.   crie   cry

Today I scored ☐ out of 8.

Week 8 — Day 2

Put a ✔ in the box if the word is spelt correctly.
Put a ✘ if it is not spelt correctly.

wor ✘

1. storm
2. worthog
3. award
4. tharn
5. worrm
6. reward
7. hawk
8. wawning
9. towords
10. swarm

Today I scored [ ] out of 10.

Week 8 — Day 3

Look at the pictures. Fill in the missing letters in each word.

do..d..g..e..

1  ....og

2 vi....la....e

3  fu....g....

4 ....a....ician

5 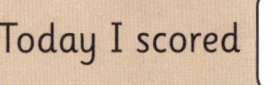 sl....d....e

6  ....ack....t

7 l....r....e

8  r....g....

9 ....i....s....w

10 ....in....e....bread

Today I scored ☐ out of 10.

Week 8 — Day 4

Add '**s**' or '**es**' to the word in bold. Write the new word on the line.

The **pony** trot.

...ponies...

1) Ellie **try** to balance. ....

2) Tina **spray** water everywhere. ....

3) Chris **fly** through the air. ....

4) He **love** swinging about. ....

5) Kwame **cycle** past quickly. ....

6) He **worry** he might fall off. ....

7) Hector **copy** Wendy the clown. ....

8) Hector **annoy** Wendy. ....

Today I scored ☐ out of 8.

Week 8 — Day 5

Write the correct spelling of each word in bold to complete the crossword.

Across

1) Viv was **unabel** to finish the test.

2) Tia couldn't **unndo** her laces.

4) Broccoli cake tastes **uunusual**.

5) Please can you **unnlock** the door?

Down

3) The boy's teasing is **unkkind**.

4) Patricia felt really **unnwel**.

6) We'll be late **unles** we run!

Today I scored ☐ out of 7.

Week 9 — Day 1

Put a ✔ in the box if the word in bold is spelt correctly.
Put a ✘ if the word in bold is not spelt correctly.

We live in the **contryside**. ✘

① My dad is digging with a **shuvel**. ☐

② Mum wears **gloves** in the garden. ☐

③ We have a **couple** of chickens. ☐

④ The hens laid a **douzen** eggs. ☐

⑤ Our pigs play in the **moud**. ☐

⑥ We'll have to give them **another** bath! ☐

⑦ A **dove** is hiding from the cat. ☐

⑧ The cat is in **truble** for chasing it. ☐

Today I scored ☐ out of 8.

Week 9 — Day 2

Colour the picture next to the word that is spelt correctly.  vijion | vision

1)  treasure | treazure

2)  leishure | leisure

3)  explozzion | explosion

4)  measure | measjure

5)  divishion | division

6)  television | televizion

Today I scored ☐ out of 6.

Week 9 — Day 3

Read each sentence. Circle the letters missing from the word in bold.

Helen stepped into the **w___drobe**. | or | (ar) |

1. She was in another **w___ld**! | or | ar |

2. She was inside a **w___kshop**. | or | ar |

3. A **dw___f** welcomed her. | or | ar |

4. He had a **w___t** on his nose. | or | ar |

5. "You have a chance to win a great **aw___d**," he said. | or | ar |

6. "It will be tricky," he **w___ned**. | or | ar |

7. "You can only win if you are **w___thy**!" | or | ar |

Today I scored ☐ out of 7.

Week 9 — Day 4

Draw lines between the letters in each box to spell a word. The first letter of the word is red. Use the picture to help you.

1.

| m | o | u |
| e | | s |

2.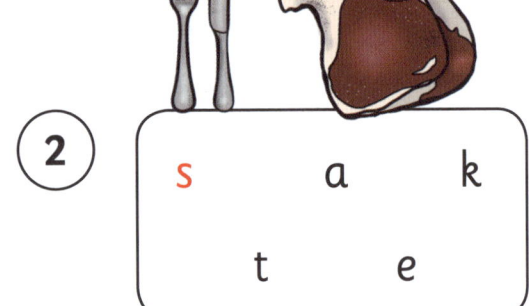

| s | a | k |
| t | | e |

3.

| h | o | s |
| u | | e |

4.

| w | a | r |
| t | | e |

5.

| f | r | n |
| i | e | d |

6.

| s | l | o |
| c | h | o |

Today I scored ☐ out of 6.

Week 9 — Day 5

Look at the picture. The sentences describe what is happening. Write the correct spelling of the words in bold.

1. Jason **wallks** his dog in the park. ....

2. Salima **talkks** to Amy. ....

3. Ryan has **falen** over. ....

4. His mum **allways** looks after him. ....

5. Raj **cals** to his friend. ....

6. The **smal** bird sings loudly. ....

Today I scored [ ] out of 6.

Week 10 — Day 2

Read each sentence. Circle 'yes' or 'no' to show whether the word in bold is spelt correctly.

Lola **wos** tired.

yes | **no** (circled)

1. Ned **washes** his hair.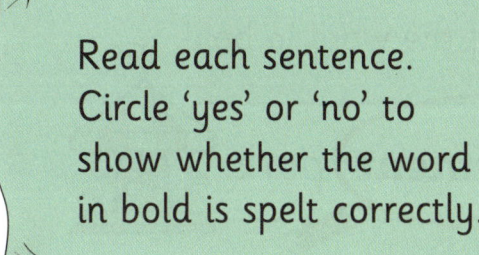

   yes | no

2. Ana puts on some **socks**.

   yes | no

3. Cai eats a **woffle** for breakfast.

   yes | no

4. Obuya drinks some **squash**.

   yes | no

5. Liam **mops** the floor.

   yes | no

6. Josie goes to the **shaps**.

   yes | no

7. Gerard **wonts** some chocolate.

   yes | no

8. Briony **knocks** on the door.

   yes | no

Today I scored ☐ out of 8.

Week 10 — Day 3

Read each sentence. Circle the correct spelling of the word in bold.

Kit was at an **amusment** / **(amusement)** park.

1. The rides gave him great **enjoyment** / **enjoyyment** .

2. He went to get a **refreshmennt** / **refreshment** .

3. As he made his **paymentt** / **payment** , he heard a noise.

4. He saw **movement** / **movment** nearby.

5. Kit gasped in **amazeement** / **amazement** at a bright green dragon!

6. He couldn't contain his **excitement** / **excitment** .

7. "What an odd **development** / **developmment** !"

8. He was filled with **disappointmnt** / **disappointment** when he realised it was a costume.

Today I scored ☐ out of 8.

Week 10 — Day 4

Read each sentence. Fill in the gap with either '**y**' or '**ey**'.  My shoes are very smell..y.. .

1) The donk...... eats some grass.

 2) They fr...... eggs for breakfast.

3) Niamh saves her pocket mon...... .

 4) Smoke comes out of the chimn...... .

5) Karen's favourite food is jell...... .

 6) Jack invited me to his part...... .

7) I really enjoyed m......self.

 8) Lots of sheep live in our vall...... .

9) We took the ferr...... to Ireland.

Today I scored ☐ out of 9.

Week 10 — Day 5

Look at the word in the first box. Write the correct spelling of the word when the suffix in the second box is added to it.

jog + ing

......jogging......

1) hop + ed

2) skip + ing

3) sport + y

4) win + er

5) throw + ing

6) slow + est

7) tug + ed

8) big + est

9) spin + ing

10) run + er

Today I scored ☐ out of 10.

Week 11 — Day 1

Add either 'ow' or 'ou' to the words in bold to complete the sentences.

I can **c..ou..nt** to ten.

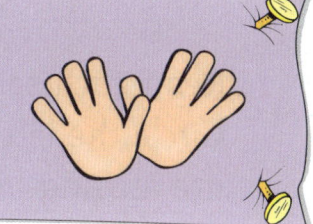

1)  That **.......l** is reading a book.

2) Tigers can **gr.......l** very loudly.

3)  "I like your pink **tr.......sers**."

4) Water comes out of the **sp.......t**.

5)  When Dad gets cross, he **fr.......ns**.

6) "How high can you **b.......nce** a basketball?"

7)  That pig is wiggling its **sn.......t**.

8) Let's sit by the **f.......ntain** at lunchtime.

Today I scored ☐ out of 8.

Week 11 — Day 2

Read each sentence. Circle the letters that are missing from the word in bold.

I've had my car for many **y___s**.

ear ~~(circled)~~   air   are

1) I always take very good **c___** of it.

ear   air   are

2) Still, it needs some **rep___s**.

ear   air   are

3) The mechanic **st___s** at it.

ear   air   are

4) He is amazed because it is unusual and **r___**.

ear   air   are

5) "I **f___** it will cost a lot to fix," he says.

ear   air   are

6) But he tells me his price is very **f___**.

ear   air   are

Today I scored ☐ out of 6.

Week 11 — Day 3

Write the correct spelling of each word.

gurm
......germ......

1. gerl
....

2. thurd
....

3. hirt
....

4. berning
....

5. churp
....

6. nerse
....

7. purfect
....

8. pirson
....

Today I scored ☐ out of 8.

Week 11 — Day 4

Add the suffix to the word in bold. Write the new word on the line.

Today is [**sunny** + er] ...sunnier... than yesterday.

1) We [**stay** + ed] .... in a tent.

2) This game is [**easy** + er] .... to play.

3) The bus is [**delay** + ed] ....

4) The chicks feel [**safe** + est] .... in the nest.

5) My sister Annie is [**study** + ing] .... a lot.

6) Yagoda wakes up [**early** + er] .... than me.

7) I am [**move** + ing] .... house today.

8) This is the river's [**wide** + est] .... point.

Today I scored ☐ out of 8.

Week 11 — Day 5

Look at the pictures. Fill in the missing letters in each word.

s .u.. m .m.. e r

1) g .... v e

2) p ..... p ..... y

3) s h ..... v ..... l

4) w ..... r ..... y

5) d .... b l e

6) r .... b ..... r

7) b ..... n ....

8) m .... e r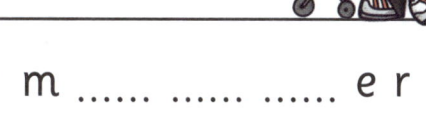

Today I scored ☐ out of 8.

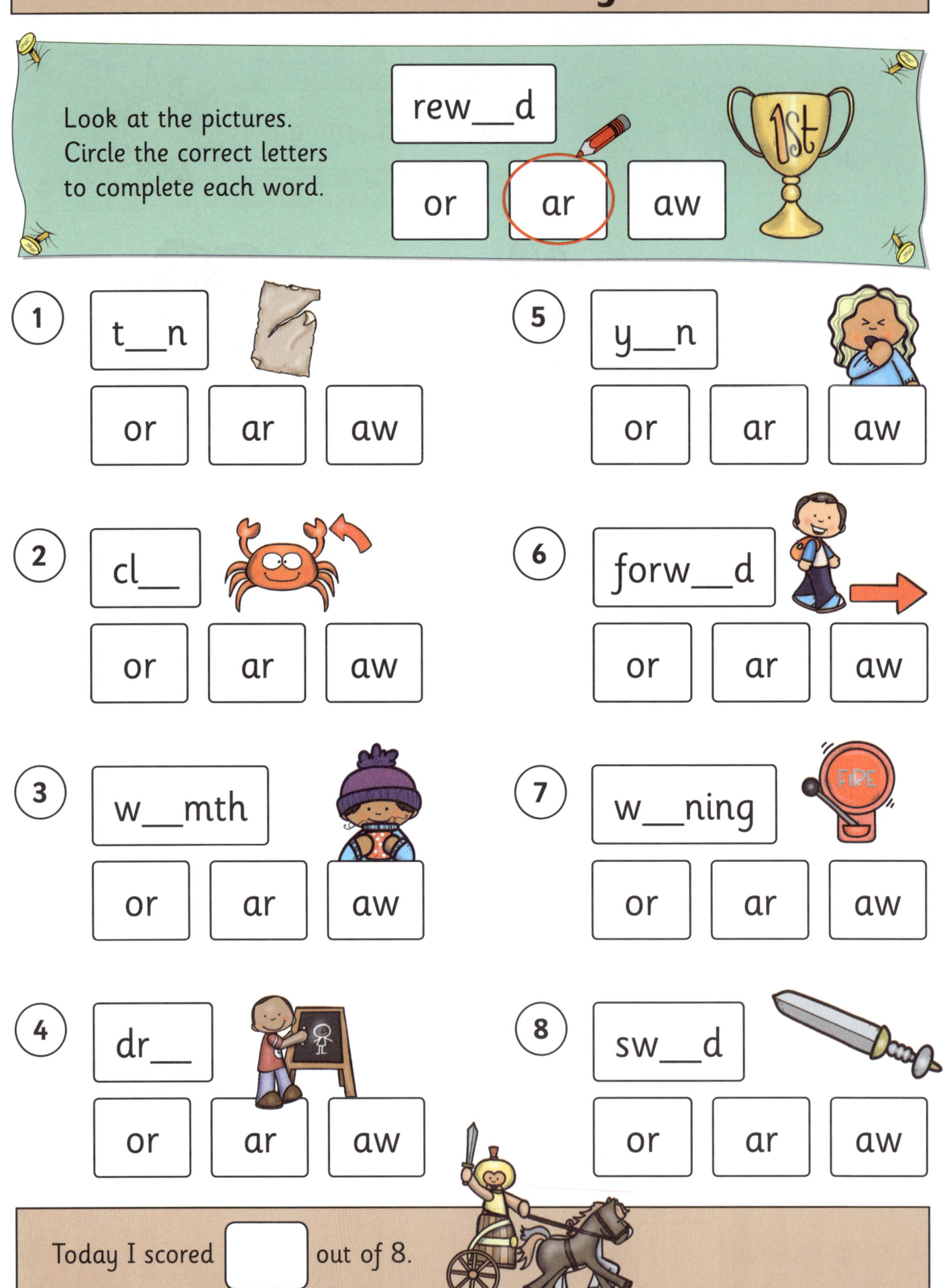

Week 12 — Day 2

Read each sentence. Circle the correct spelling of the word in bold.

I **measured** / **meazured** the square.

1. Amma could not make a **decission** / **decision**.

2. Gina was sad about the bakery's **closure** / **clozure**.

3. It's a **pleasure** / **pleassure** to finally meet you.

4. Cora went on a **leizurely** / **leisurely** stroll.

5. There was a **collizion** / **collision** at the funfair yesterday morning.

6. India is a country in **Ashia** / **Asia**.

Today I scored ☐ out of 6.

Week 12 — Day 3

Add '**s**' or '**es**' to the words in the boxes to complete the sentences below.

Ron ......*tidies*...... his desk. | tidy |

1) Charlotte can't find her .... | key |

2) I make some .... by train. | journey |

3) Joel .... his hands. | dry |

4) Milo watched the amazing .... | display |

5) There are lots of .... | lorry |

6) The pilot has been to many .... | country |

7) The tree .... in the wind. | sway |

Today I scored ☐ out of 7.

Year 2 Spelling — Spring Term

Week 12 — Day 4

Look at the word in the first box. Write the correct spelling of the word when the suffix in the second box is added to it.

fond + ness ...... *fondness* ......

1) soft + ness ....

2) treat + ment ....

3) shy + ness ....

4) dizzy + ness ....

5) punish + ment ....

6) happy + ness ....

7) cosy + ness ....

8) argue + ment ....

Today I scored ☐ out of 8.

Week 12 — Day 5

Write the correct spelling of each word in bold to complete the crossword.

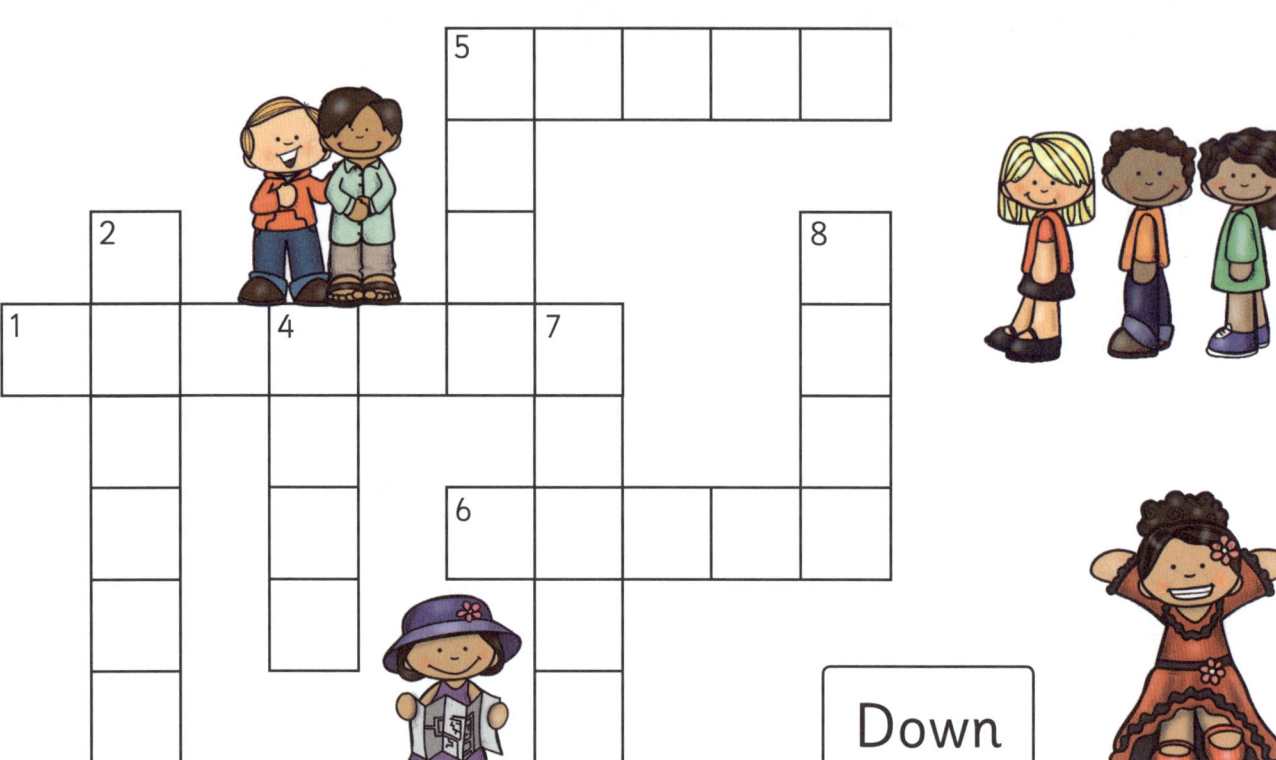

Across

1) Harry is **frends** with Salman.

3) There is a line of **peepul**.

5) Molly has **shugar** in her tea.

6) Do you know **whear** we are?

Down

2) Her dress is very **pritty**.

4) He has blue **ies**.

5) Freya **sayd** that she felt ill.

7) I walk to **skool**.

8) We've only been to London **wonce**.

Today I scored ☐ out of 9.

Year 2 Spelling — Spring Term

Answers

Week 1 — Day 1

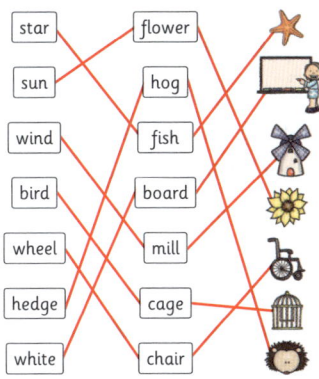

Week 1 — Day 2
1. My favourite **person** is Jake.
2. Jake is a diamond **miner**.
3. He loves going **underground**.
4. Jake found a **herd** of sheep in his mine.
5. They were looking for **water**.
6. Jake **covered** their heads with helmets.
7. He fed them grass when they got **nervous**.

Week 1 — Day 3
1. ✔
2. ✘
3. ✔
4. ✘
5. ✔
6. ✘
7. ✘
8. ✘
9. ✔
10. ✔

Week 1 — Day 4
1. acorn
2. straw
3. snore
4. horse
5. sauce
6. tractor
7. haunt
8. squawk
9. autumn
10. forehead

Week 1 — Day 5
1. hoof
2. moose
3. chewed
4. statue
5. view
6. rescue
7. rooster
8. stew

Week 2 — Day 1
1. shy
2. dry
3. spy
4. cry
5. reply
6. terrify

Week 2 — Day 2
1. piece
2. purse
3. cyclist
4. dice
5. silent
6. police
7. circus
8. pencil
9. seal
10. syrup

Week 2 — Day 3
1. I wore a **mask** to the ball.
2. Yusuf opens the **can**.
3. Luke is very **kind**.
4. Emily is **stuck**.
5. I'm scared of the **dark**.
6. The **rocket** takes off.
7. Where is the key for the **lock**?
8. Julia found a **coin**.

Week 2 — Day 4
1. The **g**nat buzzed around Joe's ear.
2. I **k**nelt down to look under the desk.
3. Radhika **k**nitted a colourful scarf.
4. We don't **k**now where we are.
5. Mehdi's garden is full of **g**nomes.
6. The sailor tied a **k**not in the rope.
7. Erin grazed her **k**nuckles when she fell over.
8. The beaver **g**naws on the log.
9. I turned the squeaky door**k**nob.

Week 2 — Day 5
1. uncle
2. local
3. needle
4. model
5. several
6. pupil
7. eagle

Week 3 — Day 1
1. The **boys** are wearing suits.
2. Anna is holding **daisies**.
3. Joe **says** that he loves Anna.
4. Anna tells **stories** about Joe.
5. Anna **cries** with joy.
6. Everyone **parties** after the meal.
7. Christine **plays** the guitar.
8. Everyone **enjoys** themselves.

Week 3 — Day 2
1. icier
2. drying
3. laziest
4. applied
5. worrying
6. replied
7. buying
8. angrier
9. hurrying
10. denied

Week 3 — Day 3
1. It is **r**aining lots outside.
2. The dog is very **wr**inkly.
3. Ben **wr**ote his friend a note.
4. She **wr**iggled into the tiny space.
5. Jeni and Ama **r**ace each other.
6. The queen **r**uled the kingdom.
7. We explore the ship**wr**eck.

Week 3 — Day 4
1. The nurse is very **car**ing.
2. Kit is being too **nois**y.
3. They **lov**ed surfing.
4. I want to be a **writ**er.
5. Duong is the **nic**est boy I know.
6. The film is **scar**y.
7. My mum is a **bak**er.
8. Seb likes **rid**ing his bike.

Week 3 — Day 5
1. swimming
2. running
3. faster
4. sitting
5. slippy
6. tripped
7. grabbed
8. stopped

Week 4 — Day 1
1. Would you like **another** biscuit?
2. We'll go to the park on **Sunday**.
3. My **mother** is calling me.
4. Your **brother** plays golf well.
5. I **wonder** what they'll do next.
6. The scientists made an exciting **discovery**.
7. On **Monday**, I went shopping.
8. We will **uncover** the truth.

Week 4 — Day 2
1. c**al**ling
2. st**al**k
3. w**al**ker
4. sm**all**est
5. basketb**all**
6. f**al**ling
7. ch**al**k
8. t**al**king
9. **al**most
10. w**all**paper

Week 4 — Day 3
1. That he**dge** is moving.
2. A tail is poking round the e**dge**.
3. I hope the ca**ge** is locked.
4. The shark is lar**ger** than me.
5. Her ba**dge** is very shiny.
6. The bags bul**ge** with our shopping.
7. Will it all fit in the fri**dge**?

Week 4 — Day 4
1. knife
2. gnawed
3. knitting
4. knock
5. knee
6. gnash
7. knotted
8. gnarled

Week 4 — Day 5
1. 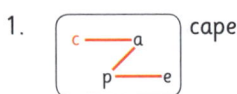 cape
2. 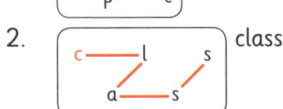 class
3. 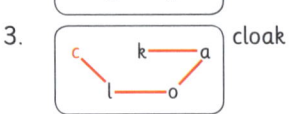 cloak
4. 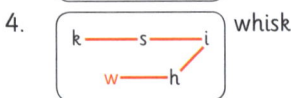 whisk
5. 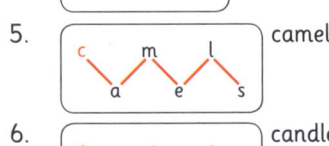 camels
6. 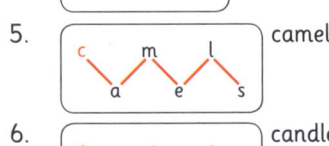 candle

Week 5 — Day 1
1. She had very strange f**ee**t.
2. They were the colour of p**ea**s.
3. They smelt like ch**ee**se.
4. They were shaped like p**ie**s!
5. One day, kn**igh**ts came to the castle.
6. They wanted to st**ea**l some gold.
7. Clare's toes gave them a fr**igh**t!
8. They ran away into the n**igh**t.

Week 5 — Day 2
1. k**ey**
2. s**ea**
3. hon**ey**
4. b**a**by
5. troll**ey**
6. monk**ey**
7. turk**ey**
8. hock**ey**

Week 5 — Day 3
1. f**ur**
2. fing**er**
3. sh**ir**t
4. tig**er**
5. d**ir**t
6. st**ir**
7. t**ur**nip
8. lobst**er**
9. flow**er**
10. s**ur**prise

Week 5 — Day 4
1. Vikings w**ear** shiny helmets.
2. Leif has a big, pointy sp**ear**.
3. Frode has lovely h**air**.
4. They camp n**ear** forests.
5. They need to be a**ware** of wolves.
6. Rolf h**ears** a loud growl.

Week 5 — Day 5

people	lyk	agayn	sum	tooday	luv
our	push	thort	werk	eny	thay
skool	said	watr	friend	were	once
mowse	eyes	yu	what	littel	where
Misster	because	speak	poor	heer	please
owt	hoo	hav	seys	cumm	ask

Week 6 — Day 1
1. yes
2. no
3. no
4. yes
5. no
6. yes
7. no
8. no

Week 6 — Day 2
1. I think s**aw** a ghost!
2. Lucy h**au**ls herself up the tree.
3. The boat sailed into the p**or**t.
4. Joel has the highest sc**ore**.
5. Samara f**or**got her book.
6. The tiger has sharp cl**aws**.
7. Who is your favourite **au**thor?
8. The weather f**ore**cast was bad.

Week 6 — Day 3
1. w**a**tch
2. f**o**x
3. h**o**p
4. **qua**lity
5. w**a**sp
6. sw**a**n
7. **squa**d
8. f**o**llow

Week 6 — Day 4
1. I hide under the tab**le**.
2. Pip is in his kenn**el**.
3. My favourite anim**al** is a hippo.
4. Lois found a jew**el**.
5. He pressed the ped**al**.
6. The train entered the tunn**el**.
7. The worm eats the app**le**.
8. I saw a cam**el**.
9. I'm learning to jugg**le**.
10. The holes in noses are nostr**ils**.

Week 6 — Day 5
1. N**oo**n means midday.
2. I tightened the scr**ew**.
3. The g**oo**se flapped its wings.
4. Joy gl**ue**d her work into her book.
5. The ship's cr**ew** said, "Ahoy!"
6. Kemal searched for cl**ues**.

Week 7 — Day 1

1. p**ou**ch
2. g**ow**n
3. b**oo**k
4. fr**ow**n
5. h**ou**nd
6. h**oo**k
7. cl**ou**dy
8. cr**ow**n

Week 7 — Day 2

1. Jim draws a **c**ircle.
2. Li flies a **k**ite.
3. Priya is **s**illy.
4. Sasha is **c**lever.
5. I play the **c**ymbals.
6. Ime wants a **c**astle.
7. There's a flo**ck** of sheep.
8. Tim hates lettu**ce**.

Week 7 — Day 3

1. Saul is **work**ing hard.
2. Cleo likes using big **words**.
3. The **workbook** is exciting.
4. That gem is **worth**less.
5. We **worship** in the temple.
6. The rain is **worse** today.
7. His actions are **worthy** of praise.

Week 7 — Day 4

1. **sn**ap
2. **sl**ice
3. **sp**ider
4. **sc**ream
5. blu**sh**
6. **sw**eep
7. **sk**ate
8. **sm**oke

Week 7 — Day 5

1. decided
2. tastier
3. baking
4. nastiest
5. shaped
6. Later
7. craziest

Week 8 — Day 1

1. I was in **my** garden.
2. It was warm and **dry**.
3. A **butterfly** fluttered past.
4. I could not believe my **eyes**!
5. I wanted to **try** and catch it.
6. It was too **sly** and it flew away.
7. It must have been **shy**!
8. I wanted to **cry**.

Week 8 — Day 2

1. ✔
2. ✘
3. ✔
4. ✘
5. ✘
6. ✔
7. ✔
8. ✘
9. ✘
10. ✔

Week 8 — Day 3

1. **j**og
2. villa**ge**
3. fu**dge**
4. ma**g**ician
5. sle**dge**
6. **j**acket
7. lar**ge**
8. ra**ge**
9. **j**igsaw
10. **g**ingerbread

Week 8 — Day 4

1. tries
2. sprays
3. flies
4. loves
5. cycles
6. worries
7. copies
8. annoys

Week 8 — Day 5

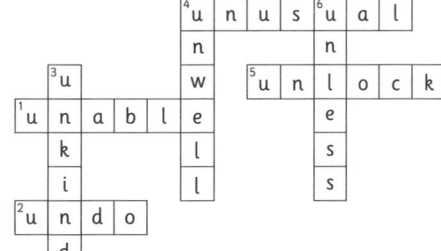

Week 9 — Day 1

1. ✘
2. ✔
3. ✔
4. ✘
5. ✘
6. ✔
7. ✔
8. ✘

Week 9 — Day 2

1. treasure
2. leisure
3. explosion
4. measure
5. division
6. television

Week 9 — Day 3

1. She was in another w**or**ld!
2. She was inside a w**or**kshop.
3. A dw**ar**f welcomed her.
4. He had a w**ar**t on his nose.
5. "You have a chance to win a great aw**ar**d," he said.
6. "It will be tricky," he w**ar**ned.
7. "You can only win if you are w**or**thy!"

Week 9 — Day 4

1. mouse
2. steak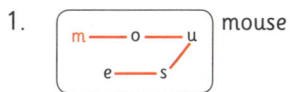
3. house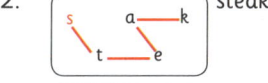
4. water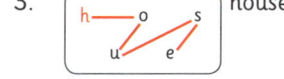
5. friend
6. school

Week 9 — Day 5

1. walks
2. talks
3. fallen
4. always
5. calls
6. small

Week 10 — Day 1
1. darkness
2. kindness
3. illness
4. fitness
5. rudeness
6. wetness
7. coldness
8. quietness

Week 10 — Day 2
1. yes
2. yes
3. no
4. yes
5. yes
6. no
7. no
8. yes

Week 10 — Day 3
1. The rides gave him great **enjoyment**.
2. He went to get a **refreshment**.
3. As he made his **payment**, he heard a noise.
4. He saw **movement** nearby.
5. Kit gasped in **amazement** at a bright green dragon!
6. He couldn't contain his **excitement**.
7. "What an odd **development**!"
8. He was filled with **disappointment** when he realised it was a costume.

Week 10 — Day 4
1. The donk**ey** eats some grass.
2. They f**ry** eggs for breakfast.
3. Niamh saves her pocket mon**ey**.
4. Smoke comes out of the chimn**ey**.
5. Karen's favourite food is jell**y**.
6. Jack invited me to his part**y**.
7. I really enjoyed m**y**self.
8. Lots of sheep live in our vall**ey**.
9. We took the fer**ry** to Ireland.

Week 10 — Day 5
1. hopped
2. skipping
3. sporty
4. winner
5. throwing
6. slowest
7. tugged
8. biggest
9. spinning
10. runner

Week 11 — Day 1
1. That **ow**l is reading a book.
2. Tigers can gr**ow**l very loudly.
3. "I like your pink tr**ou**sers."
4. Water comes out of the sp**out**.
5. When Dad gets cross, he fr**ow**ns.
6. "How high can you b**ou**nce a basketball?"
7. That pig is wiggling its sn**out**.
8. Let's sit by the f**ou**ntain at lunchtime.

Week 11 — Day 2
1. I always take very good c**are** of it.
2. Still, it needs some rep**airs**.
3. The mechanic st**are**s at it.
4. He is amazed because it is unusual and r**are**.
5. "I f**ear** it will cost a lot to fix," he says.
6. But he tells me his price is very f**air**.

Week 11 — Day 3
1. girl
2. third
3. hurt
4. burning
5. chirp
6. nurse
7. perfect
8. person

Week 11 — Day 4
1. We **stayed** in a tent.
2. This game is **easier** to play.
3. The bus is **delayed**.
4. The chicks feel **safest** in the nest.
5. My sister Annie is **studying** a lot.
6. Yagoda wakes up **earlier** than me.
7. I am **moving** house today.
8. This is the river's **widest** point.

Week 11 — Day 5
1. g**lo**ve
2. p**u**ppy
3. sh**o**vel
4. w**o**rry
5. d**o**uble
6. r**u**bber
7. b**u**nny
8. m**o**ther

Week 12 — Day 1
1. t**or**n
2. cl**aw**
3. w**ar**mth
4. dr**aw**
5. y**aw**n
6. forw**ar**d
7. w**ar**ning
8. sw**or**d

Week 12 — Day 2
1. Amma could not make a **decision**.
2. Gina was sad about the bakery's **closure**.
3. It's a **pleasure** to finally meet you.
4. Cora went on a **leisurely** stroll.
5. There was a **collision** at the funfair yesterday morning.
6. India is a country in **Asia**.

Week 12 — Day 3
1. Charlotte can't find her **keys**.
2. I make some **journeys** by train.
3. Joel **dries** his hands.
4. Milo watched the amazing **displays**.
5. There are lots of **lorries**.
6. The pilot has been to many **countries**.
7. The tree **sways** in the wind.

Week 12 — Day 4
1. softness
2. treatment
3. shyness
4. dizziness
5. punishment
6. happiness
7. cosiness
8. argument

Week 12 — Day 5

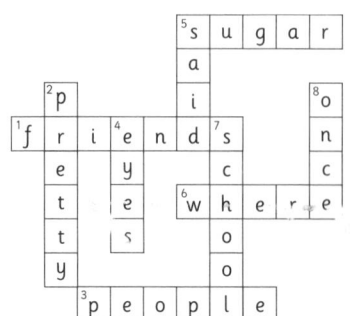